Who Said

BOOKS BY JENNIFER MICHAEL HECHT

POETRY

Who Said

Funny

The Next Ancient World

NONFICTION

Stay: A History of Suicide and the Philosophies Against It

The Happiness Myth

Doubt: A History

The End of the Soul: Scientific Modernity, Anthropology, and Atheism in France

Who Said

JENNIFER MICHAEL HECHT

COPPER CANYON PRESS

PORT TOWNSEND, WASHINGTON

Cover art: Edgar Degas (1843–1917). *Young Woman with Ibis.* 1860–62. Oil on canvas, 39⅜ x 29½ in. (100 x 74.9 cm). Gift of Stephen Mazho and Purchase, Bequest of Gioconda King, by exchange, 2008 (2008.277). The Metropolitan Museum of Art, New York, NY, USA. Image copyright © The Metropolitan Museum of Art. Image source: Art Resource, NY.

Copper Canyon Press is in residence at Fort Worden State Park in Port Townsend, Washington, under the auspices of Centrum. Centrum is a gathering place for artists and creative thinkers from around the world, students of all ages and backgrounds, and audiences seeking extraordinary cultural enrichment.

LIBRARY OF CONGRESS CATALOGING-IN-PUBLICATION DATA

Hecht, Jennifer Michael, 1965–
  [Poems. Selections]
  Who said / Jennifer Michael Hecht.
    pages cm
  ISBN 978-1-55659-449-6 (pbk.)
  I. Title.

PS3608.E285A6 2013
811'.6—dc23

2013026472

COPPER CANYON PRESS

Post Office Box 271
Port Townsend, Washington 98368
www.coppercanyonpress.org

ACKNOWLEDGMENTS

Grateful acknowledgment is made to the editors of publications in which the following poems first appeared:

The Awl, "Men Wept" and "No Hemlock Rock"

Cimarron Review, "Aging Secret" and "Lenny Bruce"

Columbia Magazine, "The Way-Out Way Out"

The Cortland Review, "My Guy"

The Equalizer, "A Marriage of Love and Independence"

LIT, "Steady, Steady" and "Zoo Review"

McSweeney's, "Circus Pantoum"

McSweeney's Internet Tendency, "Newborn Time"

Mississippi Review, "Monologue for Mother to Newborn Son"

The New Republic, "Split"

The New Yorker, "Gender Bender" and "My Hero"

The Paris Review online, "Episode"

Pax Americana, "Bust a Keaton" and "Valentine"

Plume, "Leopard Goes Through Hell Villanelle," "Not Stopping by the Woods on a Snowy Evening," and "Smells Like Every Grief I Meet"

Poetry Kanto, "Meditation instead of Sweeping"

Praxilla, "Ode to Bookstore and Dinner Out, in Spring," "On Reading the Letters of the Dead," "Passage," "Penelope, weaving," and "Scholar, Glancing up from Her Cone of Light"

Quirk, "Ode from Spring"

Tight, "Forest" and "Ode to Autumn"

The anthology *Not for Mothers Only* (Fence, 2007) includes "Steady, Steady."

American Poet: Journal of the Academy of American Poets republished "Steady, Steady" in September 2007.

The author is tremendously grateful to Copper Canyon Press's executive editor, Michael Wiegers, managing editor, Tonaya Thompson, and copy editors David Caliguri and John Pierce.

For my daughter, Jessie

Question to many answers,
and answer to many questions.

CONTENTS

Who Said

Key

Some half the poems in this book
from an iconic work a way was took
and as when obeying the rules of the dead,
you're right to ask yourself, *Who said?*

To learn which strangers are old friends
there are codes for titles at the end.
Most of you will hardly need them
still our life of nights rereads them.

For those of you at the brick road's start:
echo's stolen golden tongue (my heart).
For those who've been around before
I'm offering, humbly, a little bit more.

1

Not Stopping by the Woods on a Snowy Evening

I

Promises to keep was a lie, he had nothing. Through
the woods. Over the river and into the pain. It is an addict's
talk of quitting as she's smacking at a vein. He was always
going into the woods. It was he who wrote, *The best way*

out is always through. You'd think a shrink, but no, a poet.
He saw the woods and knew. The forest is the one that holds
promises. The woods are lovely, dark, and deep, they fill
with a quiet snow. Miles are traveled as we sleep. He steers

his horse off the road. Among the trees now, the blizzard
is a dusting. Holes in the canopy make columns of snowstorm,
lit from above. His little horse thinks it is queer. They go
deeper, sky gets darker. It's the darkest night of the year.

II

He had no promises to keep, nothing pending. Had no bed
to head to, measurably away in miles. He was a freak like me,
monster of the dawn. Whose woods these are I think I know,
his house is in the village though. In the middle of life

he found himself lost in a dark woods. I discovered myself
in a somber forest. In between my breasts and breaths I got
lost. The woods are lovely, dark and deep. But I've got promises
to keep, smiles to go before I leap. I'm going into the woods.

They're lovely dark, and deep, which is what I want, deep lovely
darkness. No one has asked, let alone taken, a promise of me,
no one will notice if I choose bed or rug, couch or forest deep.
It doesn't matter where I sleep. It doesn't matter where I sleep.

On the Past Denied

A lot like pushing a rope,
or shove-budging the earth—
it's tough to ditch a shadow
—by means of bob and jerk.

We are—where we—were.
We're—one—time-lapse—blur.
Our past with sweet derision
we—cannot—inter.

The thing we hide returns
—just as it turns—to leave
and speaks a hope—that doubts
as—fervently—as it believes.

At last I land—on ground
unfirm—to balance theft and duty.
I reckon flesh—and history—
as real as truth and beauty.

The Spider

Spider, spider, spinning tight
against the darkness of the night,
what inspired geometry
is wonder at your web from me?

On what different leads or lies
could my sympathies arise
if, instead of these aspire,
I had but gone out there entire?

In the purpose of your art
twist the neurons of my heart.
For having lost a rhythm's beat,
I dread my hand and drag my feet.

What the knowing? What the chain?
In what furnace burns my brain?
Where's the Advil? What's to grab?
I've got your heartthrob in my bag.

When I'm the witness and the fears
fat and lean, bread, pills, and tears,
and spider winding, watched by me.
And nature's *this* made all of we.

Spider, spider, knitting white
against the blackness of the night
what wacky-strange geometry
could frame our sweet-ass symmetry?

Ode from Spring

Two sisters have cups of bubble tea,
one is Spring and one is Autumn.
Autumn, barely more together than
a pile of leaves, is envious of Spring.

Spring says, *Don't bother envying me,*
I'm no longer alive. I'm aware
my songs are sweet and bright, fresh
pink, skipping on life.

But where are the songs of spring?
Autumn looks up, considers. Spring
nods and shakes a finger, says:
Ay, where are they now? Anyhow,
you have your songs, too. Your lambs
are no longer young, but give a nice
throaty bleat. Your hair has grown
long and looks great, even with
bits of hay and grass in it. True,
I have flowers, but you have fruit.

Because there is nothing between
you and the winter, you stay to see
that even the last fruit crushed for jars
has oozed its final press in cold sluice.
The imminence of winter makes you
loyal, willing to stay, to loll around
indulging each pungent vigil. Listen
to whistling redbreasts gather to follow
you, and twitter the city sky.

Ode to Autumn

You are overbrimming the hive's clammy cells.

Why set budding more, and still more, later flowers?

Why trick the bees to guessing good days never cease?

You and I both know it's getting cold.

Season of mists and mellow fruitfulness. Mist is wet,

but mellow means your dick no longer gets hard.

Fruitfulness means you have children. A load is what is

hoisted and released. Bless is drench, to vine is to tie,

to bend, to fill, to ripen up your core. To swell and pump

plumpness into sweet. I translate the line:

Who hath not seen thee oft amid thy store? as

Pothead. But in a good way, as between friends.

Sometimes whoever seeks abroad may find

thee... on a half-reap'd furrow sound asleep,

anyone looking can find you passed out from opium,

and the scene is striking because you were scything off

a bloodred harvest, and the patch ahead is bright red,

and stops at your recumbent splayed somnolent body.

After a while, life is a basket full of what you
made and you have to cross a brook, so you
carry it on your head. You feel every muscle in your neck.

The juice is thick, the sun's bright hand
pushes through a cloud with long fingers of light
that prod at the tawny stubble after harvest
and make it pink and glow.

Gnats whine in the willow trees by the river, a ball of them
floating up and down on single breezes.
Lambs bleat, crickets chirp, birds sing.

2

Split

We speak of rebellion when the kid
is a hellion and the folks are as mild
as a spoon.

Likewise Republicans
born of freethinking lesbians

seem like reactors, turncoats
on how they were raised.
Let me offer another
concatenation
of this explanation. Think of your mother

as one discrete corner
of a person with a multiple
mental disorder.
You're one of the others. One that split off.

Not a turncoat then, but the expression
of what was suppressed. This same woman,
your mother, who wants to help others,

also likes life as a racket
where the best finagler wins.

For reasons we do not fully assemble,
she cannot voice this redder side
of her nature, and the voicing of it,
that is you.

You are not teaching the former
generation.

Their frenzied distaste in certain directions
was the cue you used

to decipher the code
of just how you were not to do
as you were being told.

My Hero

It's okay to keep hearing your worries, so long as you
stop talking to them. Shun them like a double-crossed Quaker.

Imagine how quiet it would be, like shutting off the droning ocean.
That's how our parasites must feel about our hearts.
What a racket, all that pumping. shut up shut up

Cicero said Chrysippus said that the life in a pig is a preservative,
keeping it fresh until we want to eat it. What then is life in us?

Chrysippus wrote over 700 books, none survive. (What we know
of him is a bio in the Diogenes Laertius *Lives*, and in little
comments like the one Cicero preserved, about the pig.)

Imagine how much the man talked. Imagine how his daughters
felt, sitting in cafés, virgins listening to young lawyers. Lawyers

ready to move from mom to virgin ears, to part the aural curtain
to the heart of the flesh, to grease up and force his listener to stay,

pressure like a fork, squeezed down inner tubes to hidden narrow
chambers. The daughters, who could not listen anymore, worked
into first-date conversation, *Of course I've had it in the ear before.*

There were no second dates. Fierce Chrysippus sisters, full of hate.
There were no surrenders. That's why I'm so tender about my
resignation. Because all these years later, a nation of one feels
like one too many. Caesar was tough, but not by himself
did he conquer Gaul. The superlative for *all alone* is *all.*

Hecht's Furniture Polish

I am troubled, living proof of trouble.
From a faraway hollow, still hollering.

In the 1930s a man mixes batches
of furniture polish in the bathtub.
Troubled, I am living proof.

Huge hot battles, long frigid wars,
silent treatments for months
without a guess what caused it.

As in a lot of wars, I was by turns
bored and electrified, quite out of my
mind. Where was I but in trouble?

Later, I arrive at life's banquet insane,
always about to fry. After dinner
I see the color of the room is blue.

Crazy is the proof of trouble.
You come up troubleproof, not
quite here, elsewhere. Not quite you.

Terrified. It takes that long to see it all,
the walls, chairs, and wooden tables.
Who'll be my grandfather mixing batches

of polish in the bathtub. He didn't protect
father. Who'll be my grandmother beating
who'll be my father, my father raged
at us. The sun shone, no one came.

Now and Telling

Now I've told and there's nothing worse
to find out about me.

Where I come from there were curses
that cursed me.

Herbs and drink to drub the screech,
talk to drain the ink from me.

I've told and there's nothing worse.

Talk to drain the ink from me,
to find out about me.

Where I come from there were curses.

Herbs and drink to drub the screech
that cursed me.

Now I've told and there's nothing worse
to find about me.

Talk to drain the ink from me.

Now that I've told there is nothing
to hide from strangers.

I still live so I surmise I am forgiven
for being so foul as a bird called that.

Now I've told the secret of the
words. Nothing better or worse.

Where I come from there was a curse
now I've told and something is better.

Nothing is worse
now I can hunt, now I cut runts,

now I am the mistress of the curse.
Words obey my orders.

Zoo Review

To begin is to let things out of control.
The park's caged condor stumbles to the fore.
The mind cannot be told what it does not know.

Let us begin by calling a massive bird a soul;
each wing wide as the height of a man or more.
To begin is to help things out of control

with a clasp of fence in beak and a forceful fold
of what was given, then out the rifted door.
The mind must graze what it cannot hold.

If the population of the park took up a goal
of leaving, it wouldn't stop to wonder where to go.
To begin is to chase thoughts out of control.

Likewise, as love and birth have come to show,
much cannot be seen before we are ashore
where minds find what, at sea, they did not know.

The bird adjusts its shoulder feathers like a stole,
a bristling cape, a heft of flight, a height left low.
To begin is to let things out of control.
The mind cannot be told what it does not know.

Episode

Too much to drink last night and now
the cymbal claps of shame in August.
Had I been wine-wise, I'd
have been at work for hours by now,
but no. Television is more relieving
than I'd guessed; I watched a show
I'd never seen before because I tend
from terrors on the molestation line.
It was easier to take than TV news
whose theme today is also how some-
one who had once been a girl had
been abused. Outside the sky is blue
and bright white clouds remind me
that the other news has been wild-
fires in California, with pyrocumulus
soot clouds rising in the desert air.
This shame of too much drink is
shockingly tenacious. I tell myself
it is no crime to be seen in cups now
or again, but find I can't be disabused;
I hold it all against me.

There must be water in these clouds
though, and freedom here, and nothing
that ever happened will happen again.

3

Ode to Bookstore and Dinner Out, in Spring

The author haunts inside the stone store,
brick and mortar. I look for her to find,
caressing pages on a blue carpet floor,
her soft hair lifted not by window but the wind
of a door revolving. Others are found asleep,
drowsy in fumes of coffee, as piped songs hook
the way twilight shadows of twin-stalked flowers
crook an urban elder. Old New Yorker. A gleaner keeps
reshelving. Kids returning. Laden cart, each book
confected by a press, with painted look,
pimps my loyal roost. Each someone's child.
You'd think I rooster, hour by hour, but I run.

Here is hungry spring. When are harvest days?
Don't think of them, we have our corner diner, too.
Above dinner, tight clouds vice to a shatter or a fake.
No way in this wet season to not begin to be.
See, son, rivers, Hudson, Seine, Tigris, mourn
that human fish who hopes moss only grows north.
Overthinking our clues to what lives or dies
is frowned on by my cool-bodied gulls just born.
Idol contestants sing; and now with treble soft
your waitress whistles at a sketch of Lara Croft,
as, outside, bluebirds dive-bomb from the skies.

Bust a Keaton

Silent-movie star Buster Keaton is alive
in 1965 when I am born. The past is
unzoned. Like homes by the railroad
tracks, mixed with uncle shops and a Radio
Shack, things thought long gone, in fact, mingle,
with things that could not yet have been.

Buster Keaton is the name my father used
for Joe Blow, what average Joe
he hated with ire so vile as to intubate
a daughter's spleen and feed it bile.

I didn't know who Keaton was, but the tone
tilted older than Bogie, primordial, vaudevillian,
before my father's time. Keaton my grandfather
liked and therefore my father despised. Grandma
was savage and Grandpa didn't stop her.
Rather, when their son was beaten, old man lilted
the same giggle he gave Keaton.

Keaton, I someday learned, was on the stage
in diapers: his parents had an act and got their
biggest laugh when he crawled, unwanted, out
on stage one night. That became the act.
As a kid, still being chased off stage for a living,
he was fitted with a harness and suitcase handle
so dad could better hurl him. When the young
Buster laughed in flight the viewers didn't,
and so he formed the deadpan puss
that served him all his life.

When I first joined the squalling possible,
at Long Island Jewish Hospital,
a tempest for a bark of words to wreck,

it is 1965 and Buster Keaton is alive.
I'm not yet talking. By then Keaton is.
A year later he's silent again and for good.
I'm still screening silents, no one hears me.

Lenny Bruce

Half in love with easeful Lenny Bruce
still alive. From the depth of some
divine despair, it is 1965. It is 1975.
You were still Prince Hal and I was still.
Then it is 2005. What an effort to recall.
It sounds worse when someone else tells it.
It sounds worse when I say it aloud.
Alone is worse. It sounds worse in a crowd.
It is worse alone, on the train platform
looking down at the roof of the Golden Arches.

By the Burger King, the houses
were stained teeth in a ruined mouth.
The crazy old man next door lay on his belly
on the front lawn, cutting grass with scissors.
Our housecats were not allowed indoors.

Installed in my medulla oblongata was
a glazier. A newscaster, a caster of lectures.
A theater of arms. Flickered alarms.
Terse, terse, I now know what you mean.
Terse, from the debt of some benign repair,
gaping at how dapper Auden feels,
and knowing that Jarrell must be endured.

Love rarely kind, unkindly rare.
It's 2007 and I'm on a slant
perch. Awry, I struggle to be righted. It is 2008.
How do you like it? I never
have. What is it now, 2009, 2010? Or is it later
still? Is it 2015? It is 2012. 2013.

Is it 2025? If it is 2050 color me
surprised. 2065? The moon is a virgin
in 1965, only enjambment can make us
innocent again for a moment.
To call someone on the phone, our pointer
fingers plowed codes in partial circles.
They got lighter later, but when I was
young, they were metal and heavy,
the hard dial could tire you out.

Lady Look-Alike Lazarized

It was any of many years ago
in this half townhouse, with this tree,
that a woman lived whom I don't know,
in a photo you can see. She baked bread,
ate with two fat men,
and her picture looks much like me.

I was a child and she was a child
then neither again would be
she in nineteen thirteen
me in two-zero one-three.
And we loved with a love that was more
than a love, at the heads of our centuries.
Let me see less than she'll see
because I know more than she
and, even from here, it near blinded me.

And with virtue and reason, long ago,
in this picture that looks like me,
a bug blew out of a cough one night,
chilling the woman who looks like me;
so her muscled kinsman came
and took her away from our tree
to bake no more bread for fat men
and escape the brutality.
Yes, a wind blew out of a cloud
one night chilling and killing
who looks like me.

Microbes, heartache, and wars
give little way to reason nor pause
at the soaring wrought-iron gate
of Brooklyn, nor at the doors of state.

She was here and in time died,
well before I arrived here or anywhere.

But our love, she for her men, I for my
small and tall friends, is stronger by far
than the love of those younger or richer
than we, and who could be wiser than we?
And neither the redbreasts in heaven above
nor the flounder down under the sea
can ever quite sever my sight from the sight
of the woman who looks like me.

For the moon rarely beams without bringing
dark dreams of the woman who looks like me;
and the stars never rise but I feel my tight eyes
on a dark dream who looks like me. And so,
all nighttime, I lie down by the side of my
searching self and my self that hides. With a
photo from nineteen hundred one-three,
of a woman who looks a lot like me.

Aging Secret

Declining the dishes was, she saw, the sign
of weighted districts, but who would get it?
She, a doctorate in hock, mooned in pawnshops
for a bogus Virgil, whose hell was heaven.

At Wall Street was a fine site for an Adam.
And Eves of power, had they pushed them young
or some years nearer. They interred his spires.
Words lost meaning just as men yelled *Fire*.

The booking girl is taking two to one
that we will miss our gimps, the day we cure them.
As she guns for birds in the dark, her owl friends
approach at night her aging mansion
begging her to stop. They stoop, of course,
and praise, gaming with words, and coining.

4

Leopard Goes through Hell Villanelle

When I am sober my brain calls me names.
It lends me no graces and rates me no wage.
I'm a monster of menace who's blocking all lanes.

Leopard swears solemn she's paced herself sane,
then eats keeper and leaves. Spends nights in cage.
When I am sober my brain calls me names.

Some smacked pups go junkyard, or else break tame.
A leopard is spotted just under the sage.
Poor menaced monster, blocked of brick lane.

These exotic ether-feasts and home-blitz games
are safaris I embark on with my mad dog Rage.
When I am sober my brain calls me names.

In the forest of the night the cat spots flame,
a pass in the mountains lights the voltage of our age.
Such a tense monster, barred of the yellow lane.

Set out a tight monster, get to stone's yellow vein
leopard-blocked, then locked off the yellow-brick lane.
Such a tense monster, barred, spotted, and strange
as when I was sober and my brain called me names.

Gender Bender

Evolution settles for a while on various stable balances.
One is that some of the girls like cute boys and some
like ugly older men and sometimes women. The difference
between them is the ones who like older men were felt up

by their fathers or uncles or older brothers, or if he didn't
touch you, still you lived in his cauldron of curses and
urges which could be just as worse. They grow already old,
angry, and wise, they get rich, get mean, get theirs.

The untouched/uncursed others are happy never needing
to do much, and never do much more than good. They envy
their mean, rich, talented, drunk sisters. Good girls drink milk
and make milk and know they've missed out and know they're

better off. They might dance and design but won't rip out lungs
for a flag. Bad ones write books and slash red paint on canvas;
they've rage to vent, they've fault lines and will rip a toga off
a Caesar and stab a goat for the ether. It's as simple as that.

Either, deep in the dark of your history, someone showed you
that you could be used as a cash machine, as a popcorn popper,
as a rocket launch, as a coin-slot jackpot spunker, or they didn't
and you grew up unused and clueless. Either you got a clue

and spiked lunch or you got zilch but no punch. And you
never knew. It's exactly not anyone's fault. If it happened
and you don't like older men that's just because you like
them so much you won't let yourself have one. If you did

everyone would see. Then they would know what happened
a long time ago, with you and with that original him, whose eyes
you've been avoiding for decades gone forgotten. That's why
you date men smaller than you or not at all. Or maybe you've

turned into a man. It isn't anyone's fault, it is just human and it is what happens. Or doesn't happen. That's that. Any questions? If you see a girl dressed to say *No one tells me what to do*, you know someone once told her what to do.

Circus Pantoum

My people were existential thugs.
At circus, monkeys in derbies rode us.
Muttering *Life*, in a full-bodied shrug,
at circus we swept up the sawdust.

At circus, monkeys in derbies rode us,
while the great rode feathered horses.
At circus we swept up the sawdust,
the doves' debris and patrons' losses.

While the great rode feathered horses,
humming to Pegasus, *Oh Peggy Suze*,
we'd unglove, debrief, and pocket losses.
Tanneries are what my people knew.

Brushing Pegasus to strains of "Peggy Sue,"
scraping up ex-acrobats. We bragged as tops,
then told tailor's tales of what the ball-gown knew.
Sequins and confetti on a rag mop.

Catch an acrobat's shadow on the big top
muttering *Life* with a bruise. Shrugged
sequins; prating as confetti-dusted rag mops.
My people were existential thugs.

The Way-Out Way Out

Mad walker, career apologist, apple eater,
I am humbled in your midst.

Surgeon, with your varied scalpels,
myth, with your scalping savage,
savage, with your pollen grief.

A vision of leather tents,
of tiled hallways. Nabokov calls Lolita's
mom a great pill taker. Yul Brynner
says don't smoke, but did.
My sentences get longer.

It's not simple like:
Some glory in nature,
some it makes itch.

It's always more
complicated. Each actor has an easy
arc to comprehend: this father, these
scrolls, this episode
with toad, this with Turkish taffy.

It's the composite of simple arcs
that overwhelms
as, to our surprise, the mess of lines
forms an image at a distance.

Truth is not the same as honesty.
It is not the same as accuracy.
It is the purview of poetry.
Poetry tests by the clatter

of recognition and knows
how to get to where the platters
are being dropped. Follow
the crashes like breadcrumbs.

Where were you last Thursday?
I dined with rhyme. (We drank
wine, we liked it fine, us. We ate
fish. It was delicious.)

Please Use This Against Me

How can I get future me
hamstrung from joining forces with the fiends?

They may offer fruit or office. Or use me
after I am dead. In defense, I'll tell you
now, aloud: my résumé's a ziggurat of evils

villagers are keen to read but don't elect. In life,
wit wedded weed and had exotic bedtimes.

Of the sexton's hex, a hero and a wreck.
El Porto Folio, at sight of me diversified
and hung its lanterns. Not now

and again: for twenty years I locked lit lip
on every girl with whom I thirteen times

broke bread. Were there a Satan, huge and red,
formed in excellence, near Michelangelean
of gravid mass, he I would befriend,

because I want to do what he does. Who doesn't?
Many are too lazy for misbehavior, or too afraid.
That, I have not been. My pets have been base

wolves and acidic cats. I hate to lie, but do.
Also, I am pacifist with no respect for money.

5

Smells like Every Grief I Meet

I want your arms and bring your legs.
It's good to lose along with friends.
Over-the-wall was once more heard,
but we all go down in a dirty word.

Hello, hello, hello, how low?
I measure every grief I meet
with narrow probing eyes.
I wonder if it weighs like mine
or has an easier size.
I'm the featured creature, fetch the bleach.

Hello how low?
There's grief of want, it's more dangerous,
and grief of cold, which does nothing but restrain us,
a sort they call "despair";
I found it hard, it's hard to find.
I feel cryptic and contagious,
I'm in anguish, entertain us.

Enlightened to a larger pain and state of mind.
The grieved are many I am told.
Through centuries of nerve.
And what could bring solace?

I measure every grief I meet
and though I may not guess the truth
a piercing comfort it affords
to act the sleuth and know that some
are like my own.
Hello, hello, hello, how low?

When it's dark out, it's less dangerous,
it feels sorry and disclaims us.
Here we are now, entertain us.

I measure every grief I meet
with penetrative arts.
I wonder if it acts like me
or hives in buzzing parts
and hides its ugly parts.

O. Poetry. I want to trust
and thus presume.
I want hope
in a hat
to fly in
on her broom.

It's hard not to feel like a failure
when you're lonely amid seven billion.
Starts to look like the problem is you.

In the Great Depression
everyone lost everything and everyone
blamed himself. You can see it in the
photographs that won't look back.
So it is my turn to not want to look
at the camera. So I try. I'm wrong
not lazy, not defiant, quiet.
I don't know who thinks I'm crazy.

Hard Won

The art of losing isn't hard to master
if you yourself were lost and your only one
found it was not too hard to master.

Darn torpedoes, damn river, dam faster,
or you will once again be lost. Bargains
are all basement when you start in plaster.

It is disaster if the art of losing isn't hard.
Autumnal, orchestric, authorial, we arch rover
beaches owe our cost to it, ride a ghost bastard

backward. Lost, we get loster. Passed over,
without an honest past, we coast and feign.
Others feint and faint; we can't get any fainter.

Loss was given us as advice. Stage cast
for Mister Cellophane; TV cast for Doctor Who.
Never the news, always the caster.

Right these easy wrongs with fluster vaster
than the wandering of a roaming guest here.
When losing is easy it is a frozen, deep disaster.
You lost, you found, the rest could master.

A Marriage of Love and Independence

When in disgrace with Fortune and men's eyes
When in the Course of human events, it becomes
I all alone beweep my outcast state necessary
for one people to dissolve the political bands
and trouble deaf heaven with my bootless cries,
which have connected them with another, and to assume
and look upon myself and curse my fate
among the powers of the earth, wishing me like to one
more rich in hope, the equal station to which the Laws
featured like him, like him with friends possessed,
of Nature entitle them,

with what I most enjoy contented least;
we, therefore, these thoughts myself almost despising,
for the rectitude of our intentions, do,
haply I think on thee, and then my state
by Authority of the good People of these Colonies
(like to the lark at break of day arising
solemnly declare, That these United Colonies
from sullen earth) sings hymns at heaven's gate;
are, and of Right ought to be Free and Independent States;
for thy sweet love rememb'red such wealth brings
that then I scorn, and change my state with kings.

Drummond's "Don't Kill Yourself"

Carlos Drummond de Andrade
will never be a major poet
because his name is too long and
difficult to remember.

Carlos, me, stop flipping out.
You've been kissed.
Maybe you'll get another kiss tomorrow,
maybe not, ad infinitum. Nothing
can be done about this
exciting series of possibilities.
The only way to stop it would be to kill
yourself, so don't. Just stay
and hope for more kisses, even sex.

You, tellurian, earth-beast, are flipping out
because you have spent the night
enraptured by love, a common thing
in the world.

Your insides are going nuts with panic
and emotion, also pretty normal.
The feelings and hormones and thoughts
going on in my head right now are a cacophony,
like a symphony of prayers, old record players,
Catholic signs and wonders, commercials
for soap and better living. There's no way
to make any sense of this racket inside.

Meanwhile you are walking around town,
looking normal but with such a slammed heart
that you are identifying with every passing tree.
When someone lets out one of those moans

that might be anything, might just be the sigh
of sitting down, it's such a relief. *Oh!* someone
cries out and you agree. *Oh*, me too.
And the lights go out in the theater. Me too.

Carlos is alone and says to himself that love,
especially in the light of day, is always sad,
and it is true, but it's not all that's true,
and he knows it, calling himself a boy to hint
that someone too young to know is trying to know,
while nearby, also inside the poet, is the sublime
and graceful knowing. See what he says,
in the last lines? *Tell it to nobody, / nobody knows
nor shall know.* He's closing the poem there,
tucking his scarf into his overcoat.
But also he's counseling himself
to keep the crazy hidden, keep the despair hidden;
he says *Hide it*, but he's telling us.

It's safer to keep it to himself,
but he gets it on paper
and hands it out across the century to me,
and I take it and I say, *Thank you
Carlos Drummond de A… I wish I could
remember your name.*
I get stuck on the Andrade part.

Now reader, what I wanted the poem to say
was less, *Self, don't flee from feeling,
even though it is so frightening that you almost feel
like running off a ledge,* and more, *Friends,
selves, countrymen of the realms of gold, fellows
and sisters of outrageous despair, don't kill yourselves.*

I wanted to say: We have to talk to each other.
We broken. We need to keep drinking tea
or wine and tell each other the one thing
we don't have to trance out to hear: I was there.
It sucked. It was insane, the things I said to myself
to stay sane. You too? Got a hot brain
from coping too long all up in your head alone?
Don't kill yourself.
Come over and drink coffee
or beer with us and tell us.

People who do not ever feel this way pity us.

Maybe you don't want to be pitied, but I'm ready
to know that being someone who has hard times
is often awful, as awful as other awful things,
and that's how it is for me. So pity away,
ye normals, and freaks come sit by me.

The Lion and the Honeycomb

In the book of Judges in the Hebrew Bible
is the story of Samson, which is strange
and mostly sad and hints at meaning
in buzzes and bee stings, but seems to only
arrive, at best, at beauty.

Within Samson's story is his riddle,
when having killed a young lion
with his bare hands, he returns to it
months later (who wouldn't return
to tragic triumph) and finds
a storm of bees has built its hive
in the ribs of the big cat's bones.

He scoops honey from it and serves it
to his Philistine in-laws, taunting them
to guess at the sense of: "Out of the eater,
something to eat. Out of the strong,
something sweet." Everyone involved is
dead at the end, yet the story lives on,
the way strange stories do. This is an ode
about meaning and redemption
to be sung by the hive's queen bee:

The Bee

The bee finds out that she is queen
and knows the price of being queen
is every single thing.

The bee picks out for lifetime bed
a long-dead cat of tawny veldt.
A male, but not yet maned.

His rib-cage bone, a brace for wax,
is odd with grace, a lattice home,
a light-brass gold with honey.

Its leather breathes the weather better
than the usual tree-trunk tether;
white skull a bowl for rain.

Tail a trail of bone descending
from chunk to chit, receding out,
to point at her fields of bloom.

Drones leave my lion long alone
and from his heart I buzz and be
of sweetness, meat, and feeding.

The price I found of being queen
was every single other thing.
This is why I ask so much of honey.

At the end of William Butler Yeats's poem "Vacillation," the old poet has oscillated to and from various ways of seeing the meaning of the world and just before the final lines, where he dismisses the charismatic Christian apologist of his day, Von Hügel, with a bit of love ("So get you gone, Von Hügel, though with blessings on your head"), Yeats gives us these lines: "The lion and the honeycomb, what has Scripture said?"

What could he have meant by it other than that in the Bible and in life there are riddles that must be embraced for their absurdity with no ridiculous grasping for an answer, but that somehow, out of the most terrifying things, comes something sweet. Of course, Samson is captured and blinded and kills himself, but it is still a good story. Probably true.

6

Valentine

Howl, says Crazy Animal.
Be married, says Philosopher Jane.
To what idea? says Animal.
To me, says Philosopher Jane.

Love is the song of the shovel.
Love shoves. The heart knows
what it knows from hanging on,
fighting its handle, until, unearthed,
it births from the dark, wet ground.

Heart is Animal, Grace is
a vein underground.

From the sky the land is squares
and baseball diamonds. Rows of broad.
Aboveground are only you and I
in blue oblivion. Lost and yet found.

Let's go, says Constable Animal.
Where to? says his love, Crazy Jane.
To you, says Constable Animal.
Howl, says his love, Crazy Jane.

Newborn Time

Now I know the round clock
has a dark side like the moon.
There is no way to visit it alone.
The way to reach the hidden face
not sun nor stars can see is a pathway
made by hungers of a body not your own.

These are the days we cannot own.
Watches draped on unwatched clocks.
Heart, a horse, breaks in jolts, a runaway,
as weary strokes the treble of my moon.
Cypress eyelashes flare a bright round face.
White noise, and rocking, and never alone.

Triaded, triplicated, threed, cozily alone,
in a world beside the world and lower down.
A holiday of heartthrob in thrall to a face.
A battleground. The dark side of a clock.
A memory lapse. The moon.
A horse of my heart hears and jolts away.

It is the fabulous story of the stowaway,
who hides in the ark's hull all alone,
fattens, then one night beneath the moon,
flops itself on the deck's breast, breast-down.
Craft loves its flopper like time loves clock.
The screaming, the hauling in of nets. The face.

So this is the tidal of the babe's face!
The wave of blood-love ferns its way
under pendulum, behind round clock.
Something about you alone

among my made things: you look back. Down
into the river, in love beneath the moon.

No room for gloom of tomb under moon
that also shines on your vivid, life-y face?
Perhaps so. Lifting avid, left hushing down.
Simians in a second-floor hideaway,
perched above First Avenue, we await him alone
with food or stuff aroused around the clock.

Spring moon out the window is a pathway
down to the internal. Eternal. Our own alone.
Of the first days of his face: new time, no clocks.

My Guy

Oh little fishy. You, you brought the bottle-
green tint to the world, the blue-bauble glint.

Young and in love. This is a legacy that
has it on mud and lumber, oh yes,

that breathes through its blue-glass bones.

Easy, fella. In a flatbed Ford, a coaster
on rollers, a cloudy August afternoon.

They are out on errands and everything
is quiet. I must chase the golden fish away

to rhapsodize about him, little fish.
The guy has my eyes. Keen canoodling,

Zen commanding. Ken kaput. Fair of cheek,
huge of foot. Cannot yet be tickled.

Monologue for Mother to Newborn Son

The other animals were such animals:
wolf, shrew, weasel, hawk, snake,
always hassling each other. It is less
spooky without them; less looking over
one's shoulder, less looking on at
the feasting carnage. I am often
hungry, however, and it seems
there are limits to my pity.

Actually, this philosophical conversation
is a ruse to avoid the truth while
speaking of it. The truth is, last night
in my dream I ate you with a knife
and fork. After a while I noticed
you were half eaten and felt very
sorry about it. I woke up sick about it.

Still, you are wonderful
and your cheek is a tasty, chewy treat.
I will try to protect you from my hunger.

Steady, Steady

I believe you can build a boat.
I believe you can get to water.
I do not believe you can get the boat on water.

How do other people bear
what you are still afraid of? The answer
is that when big things happen
you do go through the looking glass,
but it is still you who goes through,
the inner text is all still right to left,
so you just keep reading.

Because there is no boat and there is no water.
I stare at my tiny baby's face
but he so wriggles he can't quite be seen.
He grows steadier, more the blur
is gone; joins us in the myth of the stable.

Of the quakiness of infancy and old age
we shimmer and shimmy into being
and out again. In the mean-
time, we're horses in the stable of the myth.

A quick check of the ocean, or any fire,
is a reminder of how things seem;
I can't seem to see them.

You're on the beach and you find out the secretary
of defense thinks calico cats are agents of the devil.
Your friend asks if they get 10 percent.
She was funny, your friend.
The water in this metaphor

is unreal because of the way time passes,
so you can't quite get the boat on water,
but you can build the boat,

and a boat is good for a lot of things
not just on water.

Will we, without the boat on water,
always feel that we are missing
something basic to the picture?

No. That is what I'm trying to say.
It is important to let sense quiver;
even in this stable of the myth of stable,
even living aboard a boat mired
in mud in view of the sea.

Who wants yet another world?
It's enough already.

7

Backyard Scene, or Fragment of a Vision

On Warren Street, the bunch of us,
a sweet domestic dream decreed
where halved, our secret garden, by brick path ran
hidden from taverns measureless to math and
down to a sunlit sea.
So twice-five yards of sandy ground
with my Rose of Sharon girdled round
that Next Door cut down to a stubble fight
where blossomed soon an incensed airing spree.
And here's the carved *4 us 4*, patient as the hills,
encoding sunny spots of memory.

But oh! my deprived romanticism which ranted
down Cobble Hill in thwarted predawn hunger.
A sandwich place! as whole yet unresponsive
as e'er beneath a waning moon was haunted
by woman wailing for her demon lover.
From this romanticism, with seetheless turmoil ceasing
wearing hot pants and panting hotly for this reason,
a mighty famine momentarily was forced.
And in this hunger and Internet attempts to act,
huge, fragrant low clouds dark and near to fail
of ambivalent rain and undecided hail.
Amid these pending clouds the small boy's endeavor
to fling up momentarily the hose to flood a brick-red river;
five minutes' meandering with the hose in motion,
though such waste I would not dare,
in his care the river ran.
And two lost women came to me named Anne:
Anne Frank in tumult in a lifeless ocean,
And mid this tumult then I heard from far
Anne Sexton's voice, rebroadcast from a star!
Each holds on to life as long as she can.

The hairdos in the home of measure
—the "floating midway" and "the wave"—
so absurd to pine in pleasure
from my mountains to her cave.
It was admirable of bad advice,
a funny measured home with days of spice!

Adams, Hal, Wythe, Adulsa, Moore,
in our vision we once saw
volcanic with obsidian fade
over a girl who is some age
between mine and Mount Abora's.
A little lost, a little forced.
If I could feel within me

her sympathy, though wrong,
I should win this fight
within me that with music loudly long
we would build this home in air
on advance from honey tomes with pages nice,
and all who heard would see us here
and all will say *Hey there, (Beware)*
their flashing eyes, their floating hair.
Shake a snow globe of us thrice
and close your eyes in hopeful dread
for we on lion-mead hath fed
and drunk the beer of paradise.

Penelope, weaving

What did you think I was doing
all that time, while monks are raking a hoe
across the earth's horizon, making and unmaking
harvest blooms? Are they not brides
of an unknowable groom? Half-blind to this world
because of what they have trained their eyes to see,
they are lost in the crosshatch
of their field and of their cloth.

(And what of me?)
The living tree that holds
the headboard of my bed is the axis of the earth.
When I lie down to dream, it spins
and I, the banished captain, circumnavigate
the globe. In tiny circles.
He, I know, travels the known world
and what is this, the making and unmaking
of a shroud? As if I couldn't quite
get anything written down
and in my house, always, the crowd.
Life among my suitors; still life in the shadows
of my sheep and son.
Oh, my wandering one.

I find myself thinking and unthinking, constantly.
Worrying for my meanings and my meals. Is this
really not okay? Could it be true?
What would you say? Could it be nobler
to till soil for a god, waiting
and meditating on the loss of him,
him whom if you ever had, you have him now?
While I at least know what I am missing

and that I'm missing him.
I hear voices now. Quick,
I will unravel even this.

On Reading the Letters of the Dead

Why were the dead so timid while
they lived? In mind, they step in

groans; toes en pointe to test the sand.
Despite traversing seas and rushing

gold—they still seem cautious
to a madness. Why did they not act

more like us? I kid. Still, why were
the dead so timid while they lived?

No Hemlock Rock

Don't kill yourself. Don't kill yourself.
Don't. Eat a doughnut, be a blown nut.
That is, if you're going to kill yourself,
stand on a street corner rhyming
seizure with *Indonesia*, and wreck it with
racket. Allow medical terms.
Rave and fail. Be an absurd living ghost,
if necessary, but don't kill yourself.

Let your friends know that something has
passed, or be glad they've guessed.
But don't kill yourself. If you stay, but are
bat crazy, you will batter their hearts
in blooming scores of anguish; but kill
yourself, and hundreds of other people die.

Poison yourself, it poisons the well;
shoot yourself, it cracks the biodome.
I will give badges to everyone who's figured
this out about suicide, and hence
refused it. I am grateful. Stay. Thank
you for staying. Please stay. You
are my hero for staying. I know
about it, and am grateful you stay.

Eat a doughnut. Rhyme *opus* with *lotus*.
Rope is bogus, psychosis. Stay.
Hocus Pocus. Hocus Pocus.
Don't kill yourself. I won't either.

Men Wept

Socrates sent the women away so he could die
without the sound of weeping. The men wept.

In the painting by Jacques-Louis David,
Socrates sits up, points a finger skyward,
and reaches for the hemlock cup. His wife,

Xanthippe (I think of them as Zan and Sock),
is in the David picture, too, doing her thing
for the scene: being sent away.

She is far down the hallway and last. The rest
have turned left, headed up steps and out.

She looks back, like a lot of wives,
she'd been a pillar, and also a salt tart.
She holds up a hand goodbye.

He's preparing to assault himself. She's younger
than him. They have little children.

They are likely still fucking, if we allow the phrase
to undergo a deep devaluation while still
meaning something. That's philosophy.

Recall Sock's parable of us all four-legged,
two-headed, and self-in-love? Such tenderness.

Then think of Zan, once enrapt in great-robed
arms, now divested. Sock told Xenophon

he didn't fight at his trial to avoid getting old.
From the vantage of love it seems
wrong to be so full of exit wisdom.

Down the hall, her palm is a twin of his hand,
his a tweaked fist, one finger up.
Posed like a habit but hard like a rock.

He points to indicate a rise up to the Good,
her hand is a presentation, like a message. Stop.

Don't drink the hemlock. What if, instead,
after his leg braces are off, and he has rubbed
his leg and observed the congruence of pain

and pleasure, but before he is offered the cup,
what if the prison is infested with a hundred bees?

The guard darts for the door, the menaced
guests gasp, yelp, and flee the scene.
Socrates is stung on the leg and when he bends

to see it, a buzz invades his ear, he swats, runs
out the door and home. Quiet now, he minds

the orchards and is soon locally known for his
figs. Back from the trees every night he finds her
filling their glasses, squinting into the setting
sun at the door—she raises a hand to greet him.

8

Forest

Dear Red, It is coming up on a year
you've been sitting on my bookshelf
a scarlet raven. Craven. Deared, a ghost
as guest, and me, as host, aghast.

Forest endeared. For Ess and Dear Red.
Baffled queen, tattoos and nose ring.
I believed the red. You believed the red?
I did. You are thin. Since July 26.
A nod, a calculation. Since July 26.

Praise and ruby port, neither last
on the sidewalk in the rain. You'd think
they'd stain, or linger, but they don't.
Precision is one answer to anything.

Meditation instead of Sweeping

The leaves on this balcony
perform the avalanche that comes
like gray hair, from underneath.
From under snow, leaves fall up.

We brush with our hands, not having
a rake. Proper. Not having
a proper rake. This balcony
is our terrace, three men long
but only one arm wide. April
thaws brown leaves into bold focus.

The balcony is a line drawn down
the back of our apartment, greened
by sham turf we unrolled. Playing
there we all roll back and forth
like marbles in a groove, unable to swap
spots. Our rolling shreds leaves,
leaves shred on us. Later, unseen,
we draw shreds into our rooms.
How long before one reaches the far
wall within and will it ping
when it queens?

Yes. Ten hundred pings.
Then the question is how high
the leaf drifts grow inside.
What once was home shows
its inner ghost town to the sky.

Down the Stairs and out the Door

Because I was a product of shock,
a burden like a monument, boring
down in a fire of self-fury and error
wanting to die, even long after
gone of there it never stopped
echoing of endlessness.

I was adventurous, also in agony wanting
to die to break the pain. Hold an anvil
to your chest and forget how to open
your arms. The way to put it down
is to lie down on the ground.
Go all down and be done.

The man in the chair asks, "Why
do *you* want to die? *They* did this
to you." Mouth answers, "Because
I can't bear the self-revile."

Now I see what happened and I am airy.
I don't have to keep pretending anything.
I've told and there's nothing worse
you could find out about me.

On television raunch-mouthed adolescent
men, when they get a daughter, won't let
anyone talk that way around her. A thug,
you'd say, a dees dems dohs, yet he

knows if you curse a lot to a little girl,
calling grandma a cunt for instance,
she grows up knowing herself only
as a worthless fissure in the universe
where everything falls through, all day.

Curses cast spells and are curses

are curses. A hole falls through a hole.
Curses are what happened.
It happened. It wasn't my fault. It's over.

Scholar, Glancing up from Her Cone of Light

What? Is it night again?
Another day into the desk's grain ground?
All day with the Swedish queen Matilda
who reigned her reign though husband,
father, son (all decent claim to power)
predeceased her? She claimed three
crowns. My tea is cold. Across the street,
the neighbors have come home.

Passage

To begin is to let things out of control.

A quick check of the ocean, or any fire,
is a reminder of how things seem.

I can't seem to see them.

Even living aboard a boat mired
in mud in view of the sea.

Unripe berries blasted by frost,
this universe is marked by dross,
it is an essence of wasteful, fully wasted.
It wastes and wastes.
To begin is to chase thoughts out of control.
Mary, Mary, quite contrary, this (to my own
surprise) is how my garden grows.
Lamentations also are the season
and necessary to breathe the needed song.

Buzzing bees, in carcass honey,
blindness, murder, suicide.
Who wants yet another world?
It's enough already.
[On Friday nights add here:
We have this one and we hardly use it.]

To begin is to let things go.

9

The Thesis Is That There Was a Beginning

In the begin there was heaven and earth
but the earth was void and darkness had the sea.
When there was light it was good.

The waters gathered together and dry land appeared.
The waters swarmed with living creatures,
sea monsters. On earth, every creature that creepeth.
Fill the waters, fill the earth.

Bring forth the living creature, creeping thing,
I have given you every seed upon the face of the earth.

Finished, the host of them. Rested.
These are the generations of heaven and earth.

*

Good people of Yeshiva University
and the Foundation for Jewish Culture,

you ask me for a poem in conversation
with an art installation by Alan Berliner

on the theme of Genesis, as in:
In the begin.

There was light. It was good,
but there was also a lot of darkness.

*

The art I'm responding to is seven
TV screens, each showing one word
from Genesis in somewhat random order.
The phrase showing when I took a photograph
was: *The earth was an open living seed.*

In this flicker poetry, when a monitor
lands on the word *God,*
the serene black screen flashes bright white
in your mellowed, museum eyes,
crashes in your soft museum ears.

The viewer tells the seven screens
when to whirl words by, and when to stop,
but hasn't any control over the sentence.
You stand there like Captain Picard
and an ensign all in one, and tap the big
red and green buttons.

*

In the begin there is darkness,
then there is some kind of light.

Then a kind of darkness again.

Then light. In the end there will be
darkness again

and then light.
This flickering is like a candle

sputtering, pretty and frightening.

*

The earth was an open living seed.

There are millions of sea creatures
and millions of stars in the galaxy
and millions of galaxies.
There are billions of years.

*

Yet, yet, yet, yet.

Yet it is uncharacteristic for us
to change our minds. Despite
how wrong we obviously all
must be, about so many things,
odds are, disagreeing as we do,
a lot of us are wrong a lot of the time.

Yet we rarely change our minds.
We get our actual hearts replaced
more often than we change our minds.
And our metaphorical hearts also change
faster than we change our minds.

Yet every generation changes,
tips a flip on what they grew up believing
then sticks with that forever.

Yet we love life.

*

Ever answer a question posed by
a museum, a university, and a foundation?

Seven TV screens flicker chaotically the Bible's
first eight hundred words.
In the begin there was no beginning. When you
walk over to it, it's already going.

Even the biggest bang tangos somehow
with others—say, a former and another after.

*

When a screen flashes *God* and thunder
crashes, it is an interruption.

I was trying to think.
Hoping the text might be oracular
for me, hoping for ideas to help me.

We are Diaspora and post–garment district,
which makes us both post-exilic
and post-textilic. Our late elders
wrote Russian as well as Yiddish
so we are also post-Cyrillic.

*

In the beginning there was darkness
and then there was light.
Later again there was that
darkness I mentioned.

Then that light again.

The young people speak of the light.
The older people darken, the sky lights.

*

We are in this together.
There are billions of stars.
There is darkness and light.

There are generations.
They begin in darkness.
They get light.
A kind of darkness returns.

By the waters of Babylon
and in Brooklyn.

By the waters of the Gowanus Canal
we sat down and wept. Born into
these ideas and flipped into those,
everybody's an exile. Everybody
drums themselves out, sits at the edge
of the Hudson or the East River
and weeps for some lost temple,
wails on a turnpike wall.

*

Adam drummed out,
and Eve drummed out, too.

*

All of us so tired.
With or without the Holocaust.

An unusually ancient
people, within a century
of an attempt at our eradication
on a scale beyond scale.
It makes you sad. Ask
any Ute or an Inuit.

This is a very strange land
between Proxima Centauri
and the fat old sun, absurd even.
If someone asks you, frankly,
How can we sing in a strange land?
Answer by patting yourself down
as if to find a pen. Or be
Doctor Who, looking for your sonic
screwdriver. Either way, the patting
will keep you from going up in flames.

*

I'm important, it matters what I do.
Everything I do matters only to me.

Nineteenth-century rabbi Simcha Bunim said
every person should have a note in one pocket
reading *For my sake the world was created,*

and a note in another pocket
that reads *I am dust and ashes.*

Between these, there is a land
where nothing matters.

Between passions, there is a land
where nothing matters.

Between passions, there is a terrible
land, beautiful if you can bear it, but
you can't, where nothing matters.

This is recovery. You are not dying.

Between passions, there is a terrible
land, beautiful if you can bear it, but
you can't (yet), where nothing matters.

*

The older people speak of the light.
The young people darken, the sky lights.

The thesis is that there was a beginning.

*

Yet there was unformed void
and darkness. Then there was light,
then land, then animals, and sea creatures.

Dominion creeping over everything.
Male and female. Replenish the earth. Fish.

Finished, the host of them. Rested.
These are the generations of heaven and earth.
These are the voyages of the starship *Enterprise*.

*

The thesis is that there was an ending and the ending
was exile, the thesis is that something sweet
came before all the horror. Something Edenic
before the ash and flood.

How does it feel to be post-exilic, post-textilic,
and post-Cyrillic?

It's not idyllic.
They were from someplace dangerous.
We are from someplace dangerous, too.

A world with a Holocaust in it is never
without it. I hate to break it to me
but it's true. I want to do strange things
with you either today or tomorrow;
it's up to you as I am ready right now.

                    *

Everything changes and changes.

The air felt like his voice before he lost
his hair, sounded like your father
looking right at you and smiling.

Then you did something you shouldn't have done,
ate something you shouldn't have eaten.
You are always eating, aren't you?

You don't really know where Mother found Father
or where you'll find him.
You can't unknow what you know.

                    *

Voltaire's Enlightenment was nice
but Spinoza led the Jews into light
a good century prior.

Which set us on fire.
Which set us on fire.

*

As Eve said to Adam,
If this is the beginning
why am I already so tired?

*

Museum and Yeshiva University,
there is a flicker poetry to the universe
and it had already started when we

got here. Yet we can star in it,
standing there like Captain Picard.
Our hearts on our sleeves like Commander Troi.

There are millions of galaxies to change our minds,
yet we get our hearts replaced more often.

Leonard Nimoy and Bill Shatner are both Jewish;
the *live long and prosper* hand gesture rabbinical,
a secret sign a young Nimoy spotted in shul
when his father told him to close his eyes
and he peeked instead.

There they are on the bridge, Kirk and Spock,
sailing into the universe
where no one has ever gone before,
exile upon exile,
until nothing feels like home as much
as further exile, farther out, further on,
ancient secrets furling secrets like fractals.

By the waters of the Babylon Turnpike,
in Brooklyn by the Gowanus,
we sat down and wept.

Two thousand and ten used to feel
impossibly far in the future
but here it is, and gone. No one thought
the Berlin Wall would ever come down,
not in our lifetime.

There are people born
in the year two thousand and one who could already
beat most of us in a game of chess.
Everything changes, everybody's an exile,
wailing on a turnpike wall.

Between passions, there is a terrible
land, beautiful if you can bear it, and you
can, where nothing matters
but that we look after one another
in the terrifying darkness and the weird
interruption that is light. Walls rise and fall.

The earth is an open living seed
and so is the mind.

This, such as it is, is a time on-camera.
Our time on-screen.
Animals and every creeping thing.
Man and replenish the earth. Fish.
Finished, the host of them. Rested.
These are the voyages of the starship *Enterprise*.

We are tired, but still, go forth and multiply,
live long and prosper.
These are the generations of heaven and earth.

Cryptogram Notes

Many of the poems in this volume draw on iconic poems. To find out "who said," simply solve these puzzles.

Cryptograms are codes wherein every letter is replaced by another. To solve, look for patterns. A letter after an apostrophe, for instance, is either S or T. A single-letter word must be either A or I. Three-letter words are often THE. A four-letter word that begins and ends with the same letter is often THAT. A three-letter word after a comma is often AND or BUT. All the puzzles contain a title of one (or more) of the poems in this book, within quotation marks.

Proper nouns—excluding those in poem titles—are marked with an asterisk. A poet's full name appears in each of these puzzles, except the last, where the proper nouns are a book and parts of that book.

More specific hints: The word *the* appears in every puzzle here. Seven of the puzzles contain the word *and*. The word *poem* or *poems* is in six of the puzzles; the words *ode* and *villanelle* also make an appearance. In these puzzles you will find the words *book, books,* and *bookstore*. Note that in the phrases *the poem* and *the poems* an E appears in the third place of each word. In puzzle seven, the word that looks as if it might be *that* is actually *died;* in puzzle eleven, it is *dead.* In puzzle eight, one of the proper nouns is the name of a well-known band (and also a Buddhist concept).

1. SEH APHZ "PM SEH ANGS FHMUHF" HDEPHG *HZUKW *FUDJUMGPM'G "PBCGHKXHG QH FP UMSHC QUSE GQHHS FHCUGUPM."

2. PJ BMGP "LWKYW HGFTGS" KH L SIMRWIS HRYW SM SIG SRYG MX ^Z.I. ^LREGY'H "HGFTGS LWGYS," ZIKFI QGWKYH: "FMYST'MN MX SIG BLHHGH ZLH, IG HLZ, SIG AGJ / SM SIKH YGZ EKHSTKFS, QRS ZIM ZMRNE WGS KS?"

3. JOH EHGICR TIHB NC JOH MIIL NE NC RFSL GICWHSEFJNIC YNJO "EJITTNCP MQ YIIRE IC F ECIYQ HWHCNCP," MQ *SIMHSJ *ASIEJ.

4. "EL SAEANM," PI *DLRM *TVSEG, YG ERV YMGXYFSEYLM ZLF GVUVFSW LZ ERV XLVNG RVFV, YMBWAOYMH "LOV ZFLN GXFYMH," "LOV EL SAEANM," SMO "LOV EL PLLTGELFV SMO OYMMVF LAE, YM GXFYMH."

5. "TOMW TAAI-OTSIF TOBOYSBFM" MOGDFC UA UZF QFOU AN "OGGOQFT TFF," QW UZOU XOCUFY AN UZF XODOQYF OGM TAYM AN OCCAGOGDF, *FMHOY *OTTOG *VAF.

6. *COXXOEF *ZXEJA KEWA YT "SVA SHKAU," ZYUPOPK ZUOKVS EPG

BYXFOPESOPK, EPG OP OST EYUEX OFEKA O MBBAU "SVA TDOGAU,"

TDOPPOPK SOKVS EPG NMKOSESOPK.

7. CRY SBYAM "TOMC I GYICBJ" IJE "ZYJJF TQOKY" TBCR TBQQBD NOMC I

ZUCCZY MBAYCRUJH LQBA I DBJEYQLOZ SBYA, "MSYIGUJH BL CRY

MBOCR: 1961," TF I MCUQQUJH SBYC DRB EUYE FBOJH, *NBY *TBZCBJ.

8. IJS YUSG "TGSEET EANS SHSOP BOASC A GSSI" AT Z TUKQFZEANS GZTJ-

KY UC *QAOHZQZ'T TUQB "TGSEET EANS ISSQ TYAOAI" ZQF

*SGAEP *FADNAQTUQ'T BOSZI YUSG "A GSZTKOS SHSOP BOASC A GSSI."

9. "VENGAECO RNTWT, IC SCEUDTWK IS E XYRYIW" YR E RWEQRJIK IS

DA BYST KIBO FYKJ KJT DHRYN KJEK KCYBBR KJCIHUJ "GHVBE GJEW,"

VA *REDHTB *KEABIC *NIBTCYOUT.

10. "JIBA XMP" UN IP IPNXFB SM *FGUDICFSJ *CUNJMQ'N CFIKSUZKG

HUGGIPFGGF "MPF IBS," XJULJ CFVUPN XUSJ I LGIUE: "SJF IBS MZ GMNUPV

UNP'S JIBA SM EINSFB."

11. "NO GAEFSOR HTA MAHHAGQ NI HTA FAEF" SQ E MSHHMA MNWA

MAHHAG QAEMAF YSHT E LSQQ EOF EFFGAQQAF HN HTA WAGJ MNWAMJ

"MAHHAGQ NI HTA FAEF," CJ HTA EDEKSOR *YSQMEYE *QKJDCNGQLE.

12. XRIJXW, XNJ DN JNXX WKP JERJ "JEN JENIFI FI JERJ JENMN ORI R HNAFLLFLA" FI R TMNRD JERJ NMPBJNT SMKD JEN IXNNB KS JEN *ENHMNO *HFHXN'I HKKQ KS *ANLNIFI RLT KS *BIRXD 137 ("HW JEN ORJNMI KS HRHWXKL, ON IRJ TKOL RLT ONBJ").

About the Author

Jennifer Michael Hecht is the author of two previous books of poetry, *The Next Ancient World* (2001), which won the Poetry Society of America's Norma Farber First Book Award, and *Funny* (2005). She has published poetry and prose in the *New York Times*, the *New Yorker*, the *Boston Globe*, and the *Washington Post*. She is the author of the best seller *Doubt: A History* (2003). Her other books include *The End of the Soul: Scientific Modernity, Atheism, and Anthropology in France* (2003), which won the Phi Beta Kappa Society's Ralph Waldo Emerson Award in intellectual history, and *The Happiness Myth* (2007). Hecht's latest work of prose is *Stay: A History of Suicide and the Philosophies Against It* (2013). She earned her PhD in the history of science from Columbia University in 1995 and now teaches in the MFA program of the School of Writing at the New School, in New York City. Hecht lives in Brooklyn, New York, with her husband and their two children.

Poetry is vital to language and living. Since 1972, Copper Canyon Press has published extraordinary poetry from around the world to engage the imaginations and intellects of readers, writers, booksellers, librarians, teachers, students, and donors.

WE ARE GRATEFUL FOR THE MAJOR SUPPORT PROVIDED BY:

THE PAUL G. ALLEN
FAMILY FOUNDATION

THE MAURER FAMILY
FOUNDATION

NATIONAL
ENDOWMENT
FOR THE ARTS

ARTS COMMISSION

Anonymous

Arcadia Fund

John Branch

Diana and Jay Broze

Beroz Ferrell & The Point, LLC

Mimi Gardner Gates

Gull Industries, Inc.
on behalf of William and Ruth True

Mark Hamilton and Suzie Rapp

Carolyn and Robert Hedin

Steven Myron Holl

Lakeside Industries, Inc.
on behalf of Jeanne Marie Lee

Maureen Lee and Mark Busto

Brice Marden

New Mexico Community Foundation

H. Stewart Parker

Penny and Jerry Peabody

Joseph C. Roberts

Cynthia Lovelace Sears and Frank Buxton

The Seattle Foundation

Dan Waggoner

Charles and Barbara Wright

The dedicated interns and faithful
volunteers of Copper Canyon Press

To learn more about underwriting Copper Canyon Press titles,
please call 360-385-4925 ext. 103

The Chinese character for poetry is made up of two parts:
"word" and "temple." It also serves as pressmark for
Copper Canyon Press.

The poems are set in Janson, with titles set in Neutra.
Book design and composition by Phil Kovacevich.